BUY WHAT YOU LIKE.

Tips, Thoughts, and Words of Wisdom on Collecting Chinese Contemporary Art

Christoph Noe

Today people regret not having followed advice given three years ago to start collecting art.
And three years from now people will wonder why they have not followed today's advice to start collecting.
The good news is: You are never too late to start.
There will be always new opportunities.

The idea of this book is based on a simple question: "What are your tips, thoughts, or words of wisdom on collecting Chinese contemporary art?" And while the question is easy to ask, the answer—as is so often the case—can be very complex. The question was left open-ended on purpose, and I was excited about the variety and colorfulness of the answers to come. While some writers contribute from their institutional background, others approach the topic from a market perspective, while others still from a connoisseur's and collector's point of view. But the underlying element of all contributors is obviously their strong engagement, connection, and passion for Chinese contemporary art—and most often for collecting it.

This publication can serve as a guidebook and navigator. It is a storyteller, a source of wisdom, and a documentation of the experiences and expertise of people who are shaping, making, and working in the scene.

I would very sincerely like to thank all contributors for the time and effort they have put into contributing to this publication and sharing their invaluable insights with us.

Christoph Noe

Thomas Shao

President of Modern Media Group and Collector

Collecting art attests to the culture and spirit of our time—it enriches our life and makes it better.

Yang Bin

Collector

Treat curators and collectors to dinners. As the Chinese saying goes: "A talk at the dinner table can surpass ten years of study." It's a good strategy to treat collectors, curators and artists to dinners as much as possible. Since wine loosens the tongue, you will hear unexpectedly honest speech in return!

Dr. Larys Frogier

Director Rockbund Art Museum

Missing memories and nonexistent public contemporary art collections in China, eclipsed, distorted and misconceived Chinese contemporary art coming from many Western art museums, all bring Chinese art collectors to the forefront of what are now the utmost challenges of art today, not only in Chinese but in global contexts.

Deddy Kusuma

Collector

The best and most appropriate manner to collect art is do it with interest and enjoyment. Even if the price doesn't rise, a painting on the wall should be able to give you delight and satisfaction! But if your motive is that of an investor or speculator, a stagnant price will disappoint you! A true appreciation of art also helps to perfect one's style and taste!

Magnus Renfrew

Deputy Chairman, Asia and
Director of Fine Arts, Asia, Bonhams

We are all hunting for the work that will still inspire us in twenty or thirty years' time. Look, critically. Ask questions.

Kelly Ying

Collector and Co-Founder of Art021

We (young collectors) want to select the galleries we are buying from ourselves. This is why I founded the art fair Art021 in Shanghai.

Dr. Lars Nittve

Executive Director, M+ of West Kowloon Cultural District Authority

When we started planning for the M+ collection of Chinese contemporary art a few years ago, we could note that many early works in this area were no longer available, or simply no longer existed. And those that did, had become very expensive, sometimes prohibitively so. Building a museum collection from scratch has never been easy. But with the globalization of art, and the market for it, the challenge has become more difficult than ever. There are simply more collectors around than ever in world history—and they often have deep knowledge about their regions, and beyond.

Evelyn Lin

Senior Director, China & Southeast Asia, Head of Department, Contemporary Asian Art, Sotheby's

Buy what you like.
Buy what you can afford.

Bao Dong

Curator

A collecting process centered on the artist:

1. Find an institution that collects plenty of works.
2. Compile a list of the collected living artists.
3. Invite each artist to nominate one artist whose work they personally desire to collect.
4. Collect according to the nominations.
5. Repeat the cycle . . .

Lin Han

Collector

I believe in art.

Fabien Fryns

Art Dealer

The Chinese contemporary art market is still full of opportunity. There exists some discord between historically important artists and their current exposure to and performance in the market. Contemporary Chinese art history is still being written, and I think that once the market aligns with the importance of the artists working since the 1970s, there will be some dramatic changes and surprises.

William Lim

Collector, Living Collection

Collecting Hong Kong contemporary art is a process. The development of Hong Kong contemporary art is still at its early stage, with most of the artists still very young and less than ten years into their artistic careers. Collectors should take time and patience to develop with the artists in order to make a collection meaningful.

Yang Yang

Founder of Gallery Yang

Visual art of the post-1980s generation and new media art are receiving increasing attention. Because in China collectors of contemporary art as a group are being redefined as more young collectors merge into the scene; such a change promises new artistic directions.

Qiao Zhibing

Collector

Visit exhibitions and artists' studios extensively. With accumulated experience as a viewer, pick your favorite affordable works.

William Zhao

Art Curator and Collector

About collecting art, regardless if it is Chinese art or works created by Europeans, Americans, or in any parts of the world, it always starts with the sentiments—
I collect this work because it touches me. And of course, sometimes the feelings may fade or how I relate to a particular work would change over time; it is a natural process, because our inner self grows together with the developments of the external environment. For every artist who made works that touch me, I have to really understand them—their philosophy, their failures, their evolution in the path of creation.

Alexandra Munroe

Samsung Senior Curator, Asian Art, Guggenheim Museum

The Guggenheim has had a forty year engagement with Asia and was the first modern and contemporary art museum in the West to establish a curatorial program of Asian art with my appointment in 2006. But while we have been active in presenting substantial and scholarly exhibitions that have pushed the institution to think more globally, the only way to make a lasting impact on the museum's DNA is through collection building. So, in 2013 we launched the The Robert H. N. Ho Family Foundation Chinese Art Initiative. Made possible by a major grant from the Hong Kong-based Foundation, this Initiative includes the creation of a new curatorial position that specializes in Chinese art and the commissioning of major artworks by artists from mainland China, Taiwan, Hong Kong, or Macao over a five-year period. The newly commissioned works will enter the Guggenheim's permanent collection as The Robert H. N. Ho Family Foundation Collection. Each commission will be exhibited at the museum in New York from 2014 through 2017 and accompanied by a rich offering of publications, lecture series, and education programs. By commissioning works in direct collaboration with China's more innovative and thoughtful artists, we not only create objects: we are creating culture.

Lorenzo Rudolf

Founder and Director of Art Stage Singapore

Be cautious, but don't let yourself be stopped by the typical prejudices that there would be no security and that all would be about speculation. The Chinese market is changing fast. In order to compete globally, not just locally, it is continuously opening up to international rules and standards. And there are more and more serious galleries and artists, for whom selling to the right persons is more important than printing invoices.

Zheng Hao

Collector, How Museum

To own a private
collection is
personal joy;
to show a private
collection is a
shared joy.

Michael Frahm

Art Advisor, Collector and
Director of the Blenheim Art Foundation

Be open. The first steps in collecting have to come from you, by immersing yourself in the Chinese art scene, by becoming familiar with the artists, and by seeing as much as possible. Read books, watch films and documentaries and travel to the big art events in Hong Kong, Beijing and Shanghai. The foundation for everything is education, so an understanding of the long history that China has in itself, as well as the history of its art is fundamental. Ask questions, listen and learn.

Sylvain Levy

Collector, DSL Collection

The potential of the Chinese art scene?
If you look at history, art follows money, art follows power.

Henk de Heus

Collector

When we visited Yue Minjun's studio, no one knew him. There were at least ten or twelve finished canvases and he said: just pick one. Amongst them was also the pope on the toilet, now of his classics. It cost 500 dollars back then. We did not buy it.

Arthur Wang

Chairman Ravenel International Art Group

In the past ten years, the market of Chinese contemporary art has experienced a lot of fluctuation. It is a good opportunity for the collector, though, when the market is at a low point; buying in times of crisis is always profitable.

Christopher Tsai

Collector

There are many popular artists in China today but only a few who are contributing to the history of contemporary Chinese art. Speculators are attracted to the former but collectors should focus on the latter.

Dr. Pi Li

Senior Curator, M+ of West Kowloon Cultural District Authority

Collecting against the market.

Heiner Wemhöner

Collector

I had my first encounter with Chinese contemporary art in 2004/2005 in Hong Kong. At that time I was searching for a location to expand my company to China. During my tour on Hollywood Road in Hong Kong I discovered Schoeni Gallery and acquired two works by the Chinese artist Yue Minjun. I had never heard the name of the artist but was impressed by the expressiveness of the work. It turned out to be a promising start for my collection with a focus on Chinese contemporary art.

Jens Faurschou

Founder of Faurschou Foundation

Our point of departure is actually not that we collect "Chinese" art. The art we collect is to be seen in a global context, and it is the quality and the content of the individual artwork that is paramount.
In general one could say that it is important to see as much art as possible, and to use one's own eyes and ears.

Robin Peckham

Deputy Editor of LEAP and Chief Editor in Chief of The Art Newspaper China (Hong Kong)

Collecting art
is a project that
should only ever
be undertaken
lightly.

Désiré Feuerle

Collector

I inherited my passion and love for art from my father, who is a passionate art collector. When we first visited China, I was sixteen years old, and I fell in love with the refinement and sophistication of Chinese culture. This made me become a passionate collector of Chinese imperial furniture and contemporary art. The art market and the art collecting were almost nonexistent at that time, but still one could sense an enormous energy and curiosity from Chinese artists to express themselves and to open themselves up to other cultures.

Ingrid Dudek

Vice President / International Senior Specialist
Asian 20th Century & Contemporary Art, Christie's

Learn to pronounce the artist names. You'll be glad you did!

Aenon Loo, Ph.D.

Collector and
Associate Director of White Cube Gallery

Big Picture: Strive to form a complete picture of your collecting area. One of my areas is Hong Kong contemporary art. I categorize all the active artists by generations and approach to art making. I rank the artists based on the quality in their body of work. I talk to them and figure out what drives them. I pick the best pieces available. This is possible because the Hong Kong art scene has a few hundred active artists.

Manuel Salvisberg

Collector

As opposed to 10–15 year ago, nowadays the Chinese contemporary art market is not unlike most other art markets. It's institutionalized and internationalized. You'll find all the elements necessary that make up a functioning art microcosm. Which implies that it has become harder to find undiscovered gems unless you spend a lot of time on the ground and in the periphery, but it also means that you'll find solid galleries, advisors and auction opportunities to acquire good pieces, however at price levels that have reached or surpassed international benchmarks.

Chang Tsong-Zung

Gallerist, Hanart TZ Gallery

Collecting is a very personal thing, while investing is an entirely different matter, although the two seductions—collecting and investing—are often difficult to tell apart as they share the intrigue of treasure hunting. The special magic about collecting is in building a world of imagination through an array of objects; it is like designing one's own house. Like a house, it changes form and color through additions or deletions. If we believe that good art, like good poetry and music, gives shape to the spirit of the changing times, then, in a turbulent but promising time such as ours, a lot of important artworks are necessarily being produced. We just need to pick the ones that open up our imagination.

Qiao Zhibing

Collector

Contemporary art is a culture that demands your immersion as an enthusiastic learner. Be alert to information, take every opportunity to perceive and communicate, become a part of the climate you are in.

Zheng Hao

Collector, How Museum

High import taxes in China limit the process of internationalization of collections in China. However, the establishment of the Shanghai Free-Trade Zone will significantly change the collection ecology in China. I am confident about it.

Dr. Melissa Chiu

Director Hirshhorn Museum and Sculpture Garden

Take the time to visit museums, explore galleries, and see art fairs. These are the places to see artwork from a range of artists. Do not feel rushed to buy works or acquire a collection. China now has a range of public and private museums where you can see art by emerging and established artists. One of the great advantages of collecting contemporary art is participating in the ecology of the art world. Meeting artists is key to understanding their thinking and how they fit into the broader art scene. Learn the history of Chinese contemporary art first. Identify artists you connect with. Set a focus or parameters for your collecting.

Dr. Uli Sigg

Collector

What a private collector does in a first stage is in fact a mere accumulation of artworks kept together by a specific liking, or possibly taste, of a buyer, at least present at the time of acquisition. Anyone buying art enters this stage, starting with an empty wall and some money in the pocket. Buy simply what one likes; it is kept together by a bracket contained in one's self rather than by a coherent concept. Most buyers remain there, although some with very large accumulations.

Then there is focused collecting. What is a focus? It is a core idea, a concept, a logic that binds the works which otherwise remain random, disconnected dots. It leverages single works to create additional meaning through their togetherness. To choose the focus is the crucial decision for any collecting. It is having a focus that marks the difference from just amassing artworks.

Waling Boers

Owner and Co-founder of Boers-Li Gallery

The abundant growth of contemporary art collecting in Mainland China finds its home ground in a rich variety of personal aspirations. Given the absence of public or governmental funding for acquiring contemporary artworks, these individual ambitions are responsible for—almost as abundantly—a growing number of museums. Strong private collections with the potential to be publicly respected as museums supply each founder of such a "role model" in cultural profiling with status and responsibility that match personal ambition with cultural-political endurance, art-historical consciousness, compatibility of taste and financial ingenuity. Consequentially, the way in which this responsibility is addressed in each of these important collections will have a substantial and critical influence on the production and mediation of art. Whether we like it or not, in this way, the production of art in China will depend strongly on a reversed order, how its collectors are "consuming" it.

Chong Zhou

Collector

To me, art collection has already become a part of my life. Inspired at the age of twelve when my family brought home their first Chinese contemporary artist's work, this formed in me an acknowledgment of the value of collecting art. After years passed, more and more Chinese contemporary artists achieved importance throughout art history, including representative artists like Zeng Fanzhi or Zhou Chunya. These names were repeating in my brain as years passed; I became their witness of how a miracle happened in the art market. After my graduation with a major in art history from UCLA, I have now engaged myself in a tendency to collect art. Sometimes I ask myself: Will the miracle happen again? After noticing and meeting remarkable artists close to my age, perhaps I will have every confidence in artists I have chosen to collect today. Now I have only two terms come up in my mind: "young power" and "our generation," even though these ideas will take a long time to attest.

Urs Meile

Gallerist

Besides the exceedingly fascinating in-depth knowledge and experience of contemporary art itself, collecting and delving into Chinese contemporary art opens the door to a still largely unfamiliar culture, mentality and mindset.

Bart Dekker

Collector

There are many advantages of collecting video art, not least that storing the artworks takes much less space than more conventional media such as painting and sculpture, while at the same time the actual image of the video can be scaled to fit the space the work is exhibited in.

Dr. Larys Frogier

Director Rockbund Art Museum

The young generations of Chinese contemporary art collectors are amazingly going far beyond investment and curiosity to build key visions of the Chinese art scene, supporting artists' projects, positioning themselves as patrons for contemporary art museums, inventing new art fair formats, creating unexpected venues for art, and defending emerging artists.

Pearl Lam

Gallerist

Much of Chinese contemporary art has evolved from the rich traditions of Chinese culture as opposed to contemporary art in the West which derives from Modernism. By learning about and appreciating Chinese contemporary art one can begin to a establish a relationship with traditional Chinese culture.

Li Xianting

Art Critic and Curator

Fortunately, in recent years the collection of contemporary art by Chinese collectors has entered the agenda, so building the optimal relationship between Chinese contemporary art's value standards and art collection is already imminent. Especially after experiencing the changes in the global art market following the shock of the global economic crisis, we deeply felt that we had a huge historical responsibility. We hope that through joint effort, through private collectors helping to keep important works of contemporary art inside the country, and also through private channels, we can accomplish the gradual completion of cultural construction—that is to say, aside from the National Museum of Contemporary Art system—through private collections and the opening up of new channels, through the many diverse small galleries popping up everywhere that are taking the lead in building a connection between contemporary art and society, an artistic bridge between contemporary art and the general public. Through all of this, we hope they can set the stage for a Chinese style of modern aesthetic education and cultural development.

* Approved extract from Mr Li Xianting's speech on Songzhuang Art Festival's Conference of Collectors of Chinese Contemporary Art in 2009, Beijing

Jens Faurschou

Founder of Faurschou Foundation

I believe it will be much more difficult to acquire the best artworks because there will be many more Chinese collectors in the coming years. Already now we witness a new and enthusiastic generation of young collectors who travel a lot, know a lot about contemporary art and are very passionate. We did not meet such collectors seven or eight years ago when we opened our space in 798, and I think there will be more to come. Therefore it will be harder to get the best works.

Henk de Heus

Collector

Ultimately, I think our fascination is mostly derived from recognition, from a Chinese sense of beauty that speaks to us. And there is no doubt that this has to do with the use of time, traditional craftsmanship, and precision. And this is not temporary; these are natural characteristics in Chinese art that appealed to Westerners from the moment the first VOC ships (Dutch East India Company) imported porcelain and utensils.

Lorenz Helbling

Gallerist

Don’t just collect objects——collect things which open your mind and make your space unlimited.

Dr. Pi Li

Senior Curator, M+ of West Kowloon Cultural District Authority

Collecting is not all about buying but, more importantly, also about knowing—knowing before and after buying.

Dr. Shen Qilan

Curator and Art Critic

Building up a system of knowledge of understanding is more important than putting the art pieces into storage.

Frank Cohen

Collector, Initial Access

I think about what I already have in my collection and how I might enhance and create interest to develop a meaningful group of works. A lot of research, and a lot of looking at art, goes into evaluating what I might buy and into finding things that will fit into my way of thinking. I don't necessarily have a plan or formula for building a collection; I enjoy finding things that excite me and coming up against works that I love and know I will continue to love in years to come.

Aenon Loo, Ph.D.

Collector and
Associate Director of White Cube Gallery

Quality: I look for a balance between head, heart and hand.
Head: well-considered ideas and clarity of thinking.
Heart: a sensibility that guides the integration of material, method and idea.
Hand: technique developed through a considered awareness toward all aspects of execution.

Zhu Zhu

Poet, Art Curator and Art Critic

Be adventurous about the young generation's art. You'll experience an unexpected sense of fulfillment, as if you were growing up again.

Larry Warsh

Collector and Publisher

I have been collecting contemporary Chinese art since 2002, and I have witnessed such tremendous evolution within the contemporary Chinese art community at large and the market for this field. First and foremost I am a collector, however, I am also very knowledgeable about the art market after having spent many years involved with collecting Western contemporary art and then Chinese art. I think the health of the contemporary Chinese art market relates to the overall health of the global modern and contemporary art market, and recent news indicates that the art market is thriving with record sales at auction houses all around the globe. Contemporary Chinese art and Asian contemporary art sales continue to be strong. From all indications it appears that a strong domestic market for art in China has inspired a new generation of collectors who are eager to be involved in the local and international art scene. These new collectors will help dictate the future of contemporary Chinese art both within China and abroad. I am grateful to have seen so much work over the years and to have learned so much about Chinese artists in the process. Contemporary Chinese art will continue to shape the way we understand the global history of art.

Michael Frahm

Art Advisor, Collector and
Director of the Blenheim Art Foundation

It is important to think of your collection as a whole and to aim for cohesiveness. Try to find the red thread between the artists you are collecting and the dialogue between the works. The Chinese scene is fast evolving, so make sure to stay clear of trends; they go as quickly as they come.

Rudy Tseng

Collector

Artist Yang Jiechang, who now works and lives in France, once gave a piece of advice to young artists in an important interview. He stated that today's definition of Chinese contemporary art has been narrowed down to the numbers on auction records. Most artists create for the purpose of selling. The artists who matter will be revealed after 100 years as those whose names are still remembered and discussed by the generations after.

Shi Li-Sanderson

Director, Zeng Fanzhi Collection

From the first second a piece of art is collected, it departs from simply being within the collector's own purview, of their singular concern, and becomes akin to a social act. I believe collecting can be seen as not only action reflecting merely on the collector themselves, but also as a gesture exceeding themselves. This means that one should accept the fact that no art collection belongs to the individual, but always carries a sense of social responsibility. This is because if art can be seen as the essence of human wisdom, it stands for all the time and space, and this understanding brings the collector closer to a contemplation of the broader significance of artworks. A collection is a representation of the highest human value systems, beyond wealth and monetary value. A collection reveals the vision and aesthetic values of the collector, upon which their reputation for future generations is based, i.e., the intangible values of an individual or a group. To understand the significance of the act of "art collection" is perhaps the first lesson to learn when entering the world of collecting.

Adrian Cheng

Founder of K11 Art Foundation

Collection is an attitude, a voice and a dream.
I am just into it . . .

Michael Ku

Director of Michael Ku Gallery

I am particularly interested in artists who are my contemporaries and belong to my generation. Through them, I perceive key developments of art more acutely and also see who will bring effects of inspiration or continual fermentation in the near future.

Philip Dodd

Chairman, Made in China (UK) Ltd, Curator, Author and Broadcaster

Collectors of art from China are more important than any group of collectors since the late nineteenth century in the US. It is private collectors in China—just look at the number of private museums of contemporary art—who are seriously trying to "write" the history of Chinese contemporary art, through exhibitions and catalogues; who are now beginning to purchase art from the rest of the world and see its connections with art from China. Soon, if the Western state museums have any sense, they will begin partnerships with Chinese collectors so the extraordinary richness of Chinese art since the 1970s—a whole world of Chinese abstraction; the history of video in China—might be seen across the world.

Bao Yifeng

Collector

Seeing is believing. When I first knew Lorenz Helbling back in mid-1990s, he had just started ShanghART, which is how I became familiar with Chinese contemporary art. After working with Chen Yifei, Pearl Lam, I got to know it better by visiting galleries, museums, talking to art specialists. With your passion, no matter how deep your pocket is, you will find some piece you like. But of course you need to train yourself to have a good eye for art.

Abby Chen

Curator and Artistic Director,
Chinese Culture Foundation of San Francisco

Personally I collect as a means of supporting artists, especially at the early stage of their careers. For the Chinese Culture Foundation of San Francisco, we do not have a permanent collection, nor do we plan to build one in the near future. Instead, we strive to encourage institutional and private collectors that have such capacity to collect works about Chinese diaspora, as we believe it is an integral part of building the cultural assets for civilization.

Don and Mera Rubell

Collectors, Rubell Family Collection

It's funny, because Chinese art from the last generation was not as interesting for us. I don't know whether to call them the "Venice Generation," after Harald Szeemann's show, but, to us, that art seemed to be made more for Western consumption. The difference now is that we're seeing art made for the new generation in China. The work in our show will absolutely not be recognized by people who are only familiar with the earlier generation. There's a lot more geometric abstraction—there are probably six to eight abstract painters there—and there are about the same number of video artists, and then there are sculptors and performance artists. But, more fundamentally, the subject matter has changed. The subject matter which is very understandable and comprehensible to the Chinese; it's a strong, internally-based subject matter. It's not for anybody else. The works are aggressive—they're bold. They're exceptional.*

* First published online at artspace.com

Stacie Xie

Director of Modern and Contemporary Art Dept.
Beijing Council International Auction Co., Ltd.

“Why is the Chinese contemporary art market subject to frequent fluctuations?”
“Because we lack collectors.”
“Why is the art market’s life cycle so short in China?”
“Because we lack collectors.”
“Why do you still continue to collect Chinese contemporary art?”
“Because of the lack, there is opportunity.”

Li Zhenhua

Independent Curator

Art is the wall occupy thing by Yan Lei.
We need the younger ones, and always young.
Time, only time, can help to build and erase, but sometimes time also adds up into it.
Fashion in art now is the occupy aesthetics, is something in between, no beginning or end.
We should collect the future, just like what we do with Google or Facebook, but in art, we just collect things we know.
Living for now, and being new, is the attitude of understanding the Future in Now.

Karen Smith

Arts Writer, Curator, Current Position Director of OCAT Xi'an

Collecting is an engagement with art. Of course it is. That much is obvious, and to say so, so very reductive. But the convergence of intellectual satisfaction, emotional experience and the socio-economic rewards is an essential blend of elements, one or other of which is often overlooked, but that must exist if a serious collection is to be achieved. As every chemist knows, to lack one element that makes up a chemical compound makes achieving the desired reaction impossible. Passion needs knowledge to ground it, at least, it requires a will to learn. Without an "eye", knowledge is simply academic; passion a random release of emotion. Without a goal which may be taken as the parameter for a collection, even a good eye can feel unfocused. The cost of overlooking these compound elements maybe high. Still, I have come to lose patience with the many formulas for successful collecting that the contemporary world seems to have equipped interested individuals with today. Most tips are pure fallacy, primarily because so much of what is spoken of as collecting are simply art-fund forms of investment. I have nothing against investing in art, but the art world is nothing like that of commodities which can be traded at more predictable (well, so it was once thought) levels of growth. Collecting art is a practice that, like being an artist, an inventor or doctor, requires time in which to gain empirical experience, attention to small details which differentiate one ordinary artwork from a masterpiece, and a degree of discipline in acquisition choices made for building a collection. It doesn't have to be as serious as that sounds -- it is good to dabble for some, as it is good for others to aim further, deeper. Perhaps the soundest advice anyone can give is to know your own limits and know who to talk to when you reach them.

Victoria de Heus-Zomer

Collector

Ultimately, what we are looking for in Chinese art is the same as in Western art: it needs to touch the heart.

Cao Dan

Executive Publisher of LEAP and The Art Newspaper China

A bilingual magazine's role is multifaceted. We work to adjust the misunderstandings and prejudices towards Chinese contemporary art.

How do we amplify the voice of China's art world?

How do we sustain independent criticism while expanding the latitude of Chinese critical writing?

How do we systematically and continuously observe artists' practices while discovering new talents?

How do we encourage the younger generation to read and write about art?

How do we stay in perspective amidst market trends?

To provide an insightful and valuable reference for collecting and exhibiting Chinese contemporary art is the basis and attitude of our work.

Fabien Fryns

Art Dealer

Despite some mind boggling recent auction records, it is still early days for the Chinese contemporary art market, as the market is still very young and small in the mainland. I am convinced that we will still see some enormous price increases and fluctuations within the next few years.

Xu Zhen

Curator, Artist, and Director of Madein Company

Collecting
must be part of
cultural creation;
collecting is
creation.

Lorenzo Rudolf

Founder and Director of Art Stage Singapore

Collect according to the same principles as you would collect any other contemporary art: make informed decisions, buy works that really interest you, collect artists who continue creating innovative work that is not (just) fashionable.

William Lim

Collector, Living Collection

I have published a book called *The No Colors* which talks about Hong Kong artists who produced works not for the market, for the simple fact that there was not a market. This struggle almost becomes a way of life for these artists, and their works are produced as a by-product of this struggle. This is why I think that Hong Kong artists' works are interesting and challenging for the collectors.

Dr. Wang Chunchen

Curator, CAFA Art Museum of China Central Academy of Fine Arts, Beijing

Art intervention is a process of art democratization. The collection of new art will change lives.

Lu Xun

Collector and Founder Sifang Art Museum

I try to create a type of art patronage in China that is not only achieved through collecting and displaying but also through organizing periodic exhibitions in the museum space, as well as engaging artists to create unique, site-specific, permanent projects in the landscape and architectural spaces.

Magnus Renfrew

Deputy Chairman, Asia and
Director of Fine Arts, Asia, Bonhams

Collecting art is an emotional response, but it should also be a "sense-checked" response. One needs a sense of curiosity. What age is the artist? Have they had a solo exhibition before? Have they been shown in a non-commercial context? Have they been written about in respected publications? How does the work that you are considering buying tie in to the artist's overall oeuvre.

Martina Köppel-Yang

Independent Scholar and Curator

Collect with your heart, not with your ears. A work of contemporary art is not a share on the stock market. Nor is it only an object. It comes along with a whole set of feelings, concepts and world views. It looks at you as much as you look at it; it questions you as much as you question it.

Liu Gang

Collector

In my view, the most valuable part of Chinese contemporary art is to record the social transformation in China, including but not limited to economy, culture, value systems and lifestyle. Such records through artistic works are much more colorful and dramatic than the written records by historians. The good feeling Chinese contemporary art gives me is worth much more than anything money could buy.

Li Xianting

Art Critic and Curator

Collection is a kind of cultural creation, and in collecting contemporary art one must face value standards, but value standards in a progressing era are of a very uncertain ideological form, and collectors—through their behavior—have to confirm whether they're actually qualified to become the builders of value standards in the era in which we live.

* Approved extract from Mr Li Xianting's speech on Songzhuang Art Festival's Conference of Collectors of Chinese Contemporary Art in 2009, Beijing

Alexandre Errera

Founder of Artshare.com

Collecting Chinese contemporary art is a unique way to connect with a civilization which, as a foreigner, seems at first so difficult to understand and penetrate. Doing so today is all the more fascinating, as this millenary culture is undergoing some of its deepest changes, and its artists are becoming increasingly global.

Dr. Lars Nittve

Executive Director, M+ of West Kowloon Cultural District Authority

Collecting Chinese contemporary art in 2015 requires that you have the ability to move beyond the obvious trends. In recent years it has become clear that the Chinese art scene has matured to a "post movement" phase where it is no longer possible to package, or classify, the main tendencies. There are many truly great artists and they work in all mediums, idioms, scales and with all strategies available. There is no "mainstream" in Chinese art anymore—just like it disappeared in the West in the 1980s. Chinese art has caught up, matured and on the way has made the situation for the collector even more challenging than ever (and it was never easy). But it is also more exciting than ever!

Yang Bin
Collector

It suffices to collect artworks that interest you. Don't feel obliged to become friends with the artists. They are a different kind of people. Once a friendship is established, it gets in the way of your objective judgment in collecting and sometimes puts you in a dilemma.

Andreas Schmid

Curator and Artist

In 1991, preparing the exhibition *China Avantgarde* at Haus der Kulturen der Welt in Berlin, Hans van Dijk and I, in our role as curators of the show, wondered whether we should also purchase works by the artists whom we regarded so highly: we made a fast and clear decision against it. We did not want to be dealers. Our principle should be: "Purchasing no works for ourselves and even less for others. And if purchases are made, then only after the end of the exhibition." Consequently, our role was clearer to everyone, and for the artist we were more trustworthy in our function as curators.

In the mid-nineties, I bought a few works myself, ones that were important to me. One of them, for example, is Geng Jianyi's conceptional work *Investigative Form* executed in 1988. For me it is a representative work for the experimental art of the eighties in China.

Yang Yang

Founder of Gallery Yang

Meet the artist if you can. Your perceptions will be more profound when learning through the artist, the ideas and stories behind art.

Bao Dong

Curator

Collecting contemporary art? Or the contemporaneity of collecting art has long deviated from its original intention, i.e., preserving the past. It has become an attempt to make decisions based on a prediction of the future. But what if such a modernistic conception of time as linear progress is out of date, or should have been so? If a definite future only exists in imagination, then future-oriented decision-making is essentially a gamble. We need, therefore, to transform our conception of collecting, which can't and needn't look to art history for authority, because prediction, or collecting per se, is part of contemporaneity. In other words, don't try to play the game, but just throw the dice.

Judith Neilson

Collector, White Rabbit Collection

Perhaps in ten years, the paint is going to drop off the entire canvas, or a motor is going to blow up and has to be redone. But it is extremely important because somebody has to do it first.

Robin Peckham

Deputy Editor of LEAP and Chief Editor in Chief of The Art Newspaper China (Hong Kong)

Art from China, as much as it now belongs in style and substance to nothing other than international art, still resides logistically and institutionally in a very distinct system. This means that there are at least two standards for the work, and often many more. Collecting is therefore most productive when it is mobilized in support of the artist rather than for the historical or financial motives of the collector.

Dr. Shen Qilan

Curator and Art Critic

Collection is one of the most interesting games in the world. If you don't give your heart to it, you lose. If you give all your heart to it, you lose. The winners of this game are those who keep good balance between pleasure and interest, between giving and taking.

Li Xin

Deputy Chairman, Christie's Asia

There are many layers in this art market. Although certain artists pushed very quickly to the very top, there are still many opportunities to find young, upcoming artists. The more established artists continue to show strength and maintain the market, while many of the younger artists are creating very interesting artworks. This broad range of artists keeps the Chinese art world very much alive and vital, and the consistently strong value of the blue-chip artists gives confidence to the market.

Philip Tinari

Director of the Ullens Center for Contemporary Art (UCCA)

I think people collect art because it's one of the few ways of consuming and investing at the same time. Art offers gratification both instant and deferred, and is enmeshed in a scene at once intellectual and fun, rigorous and glamorous. Placed in a home, a work of art can be constantly encountered and rediscovered. The works we live with become dynamic markers against which we can measure our own emotional development or note the progress of our lives. They will outlast us, and maybe even find their way back into the public sphere, where they can someday influence people who haven't yet been born.

Yang Jiechang

Artist

Take your time to collect. Think long term, even 100 years are short.

Wan Jie

Chairman and President of Artron Art Group

Contemporary art occurs all the way round my life. Therefore, I'd like to be deeply involved in it and promote it, not only to collect it. Due to my personal experience, I am greatly interested in the artist's book. But Chinese artists are currently less concentrated on the creation of this kind of artwork. That's why I am devoting myself to gathering crafts and materials, and establishing workshops for creating artist's books in China. Meanwhile, I am also cooperating with Xu Bing to curate a three-year itinerant exhibition for excellent artist's books, so as to promote its development in China.

Dr. Uli Sigg

Collector

If one would want to construct a hierarchy amongst collecting styles, then the most complex way is weaving a collection as a web. That is to say, having decided on a focus, to collect works which web the fullest context, with works shedding light on, explaining and opening up further spaces for this core idea. And very importantly, it is not simply about lining up masterpieces like a string of pearls. "Web" collecting is just as much about finding the pieces which may go unattended or be ascribed to artists considered second tier at times—which in itself is subject to change over time—to fill the perception gaps, to narrate the underlying subtexts and to ultimately bring a collection to the fore.

Zhu Zhu

Poet, Art Curator and Art Critic

Have your collection hung on a wall as much as possible, rather than keep the artworks in a warehouse so long that you've forgotten their existence.

Budi Tek

Collector, Yuz Museum

There is a saying: “It takes ten years to grow trees but a hundred years to rear people.” How many years does it take to cultivate artistic culture? I try to accomplish the entirety of Chinese contemporary art history by linking my collection into a single thread. This has become my lifelong mission.

MODERN ARTS PUBLISHING
Praterstrasse 66/1/9, 1020 Vienna, Austria
www.vfmk.de

First published 2015

ISBN 978-3-86984-547-0

Editor: Christoph Noe

Copyediting: Dawn d' Atri

Project Management: Emma Lam

Design: Nico Mo

Printed in Hong Kong

This book is available worldwide. Please contact your nearest bookseller or one of the addresses below for information concerning your local distributor.

Bibliographic information published by the Deutsche Nationalbibliothek
The Deutsche Nationalbibliothek lists this publication in the Deutsche Nationalbibliografie; detailed bibliographic data is available on the Internet at http://dnb.ddb.de.

Distributed in the United Kingdom by
Cornerhouse Publications
70 Oxford Street, Manchester M1 5 NH, UK
Phone +44-161-2001503 Fax +44-161-2001504

Distributed outside Europe by
D.A.P. Distributed Art Publishers, Inc.
155 Sixth Avenue, 2nd Floor, New York, NY 10013, USA
Phone +1-212-6271999 Fax +1-212-6279484

Distributed in Europe (except UK) by
LKG Leipziger Kommissions- und
Großbuchhandelsgesellschaft mbH
An der Südspitze 1–12, 04579 Espenhain (near Leipzig), DE
Phone +49-34206-65107 Fax +49-34206-651732